Can You Find It?

By Tony Suarez

Illustrated by Michael Weber

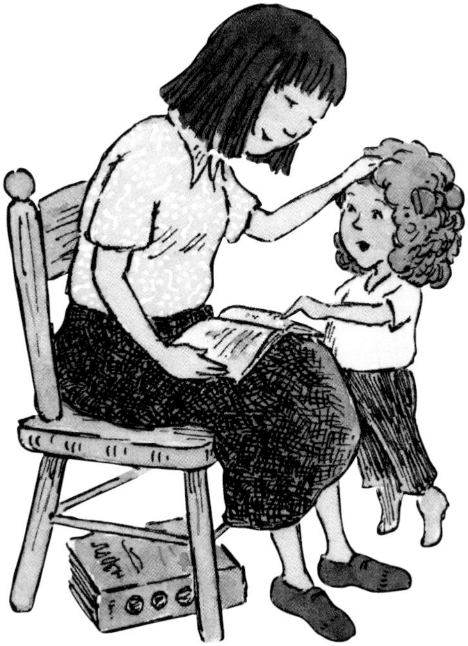

Target Skill Positions

Scott Foresman
is an imprint of

PEARSON

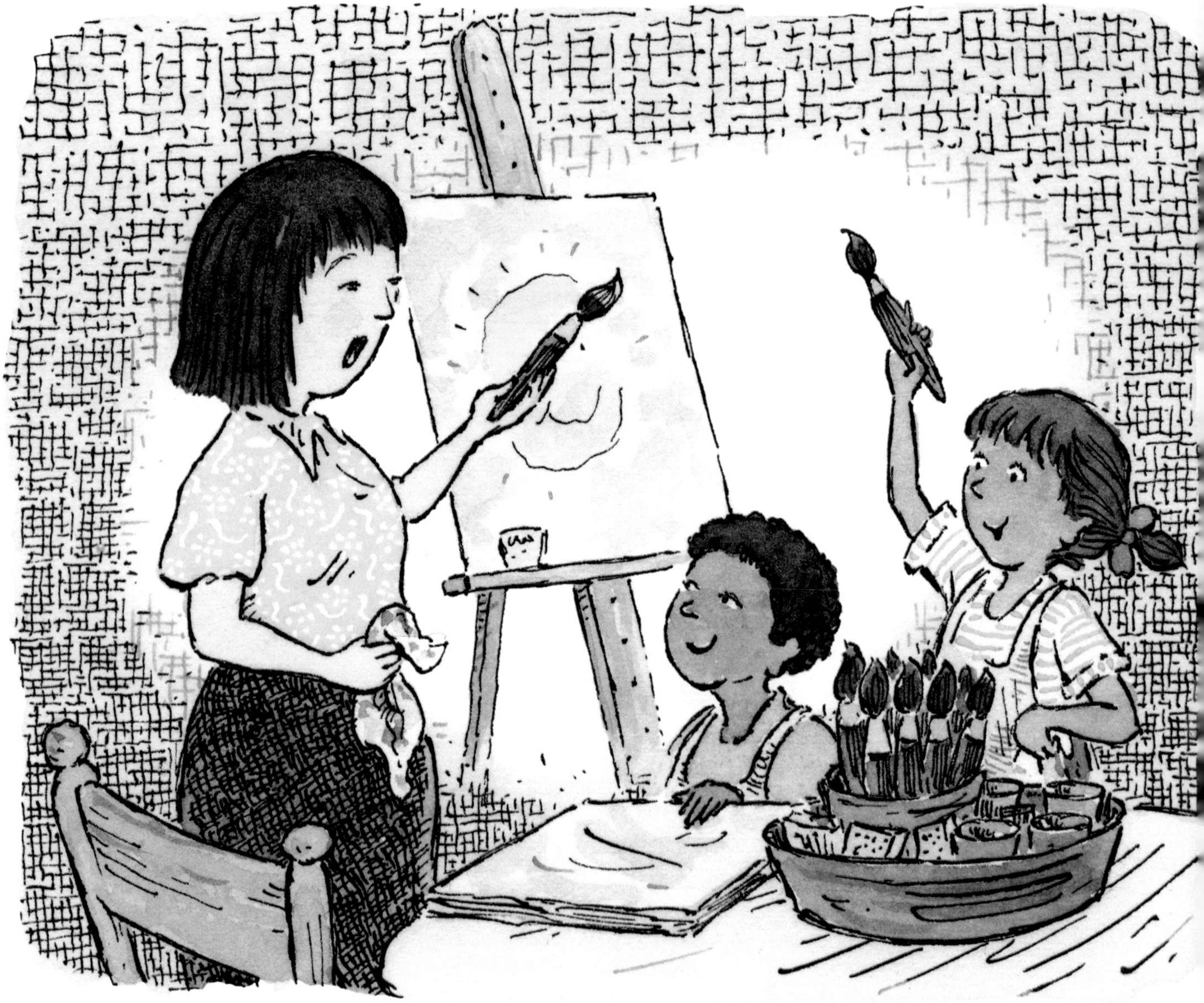

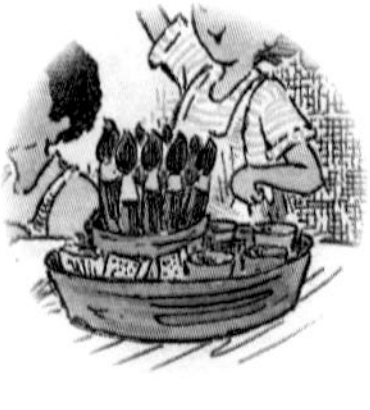

in

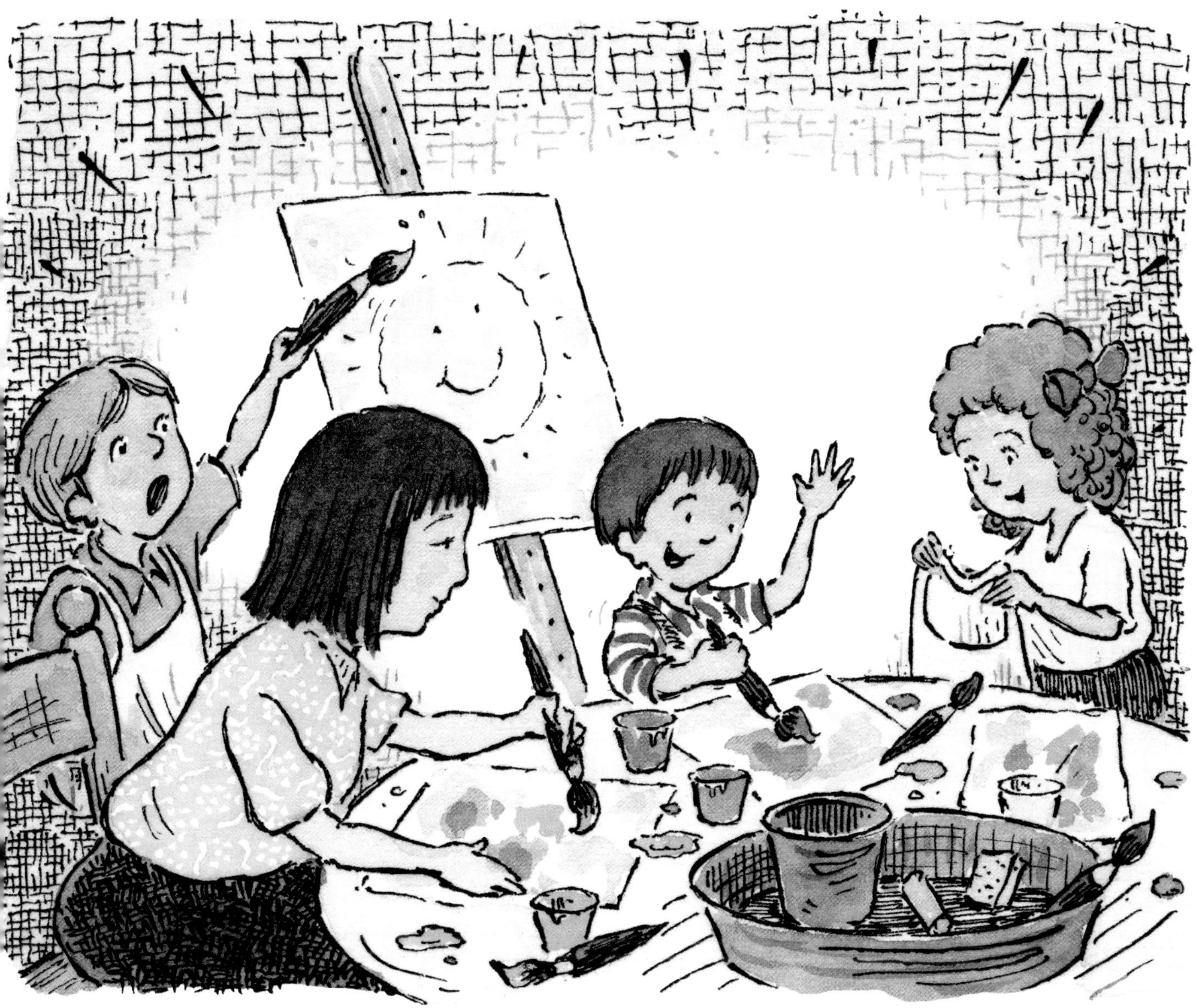

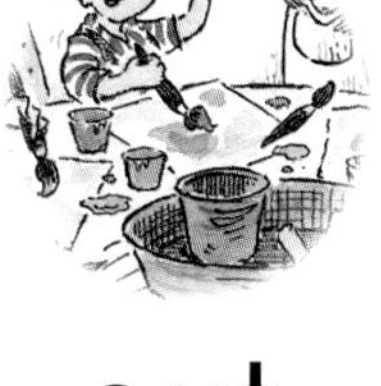

out

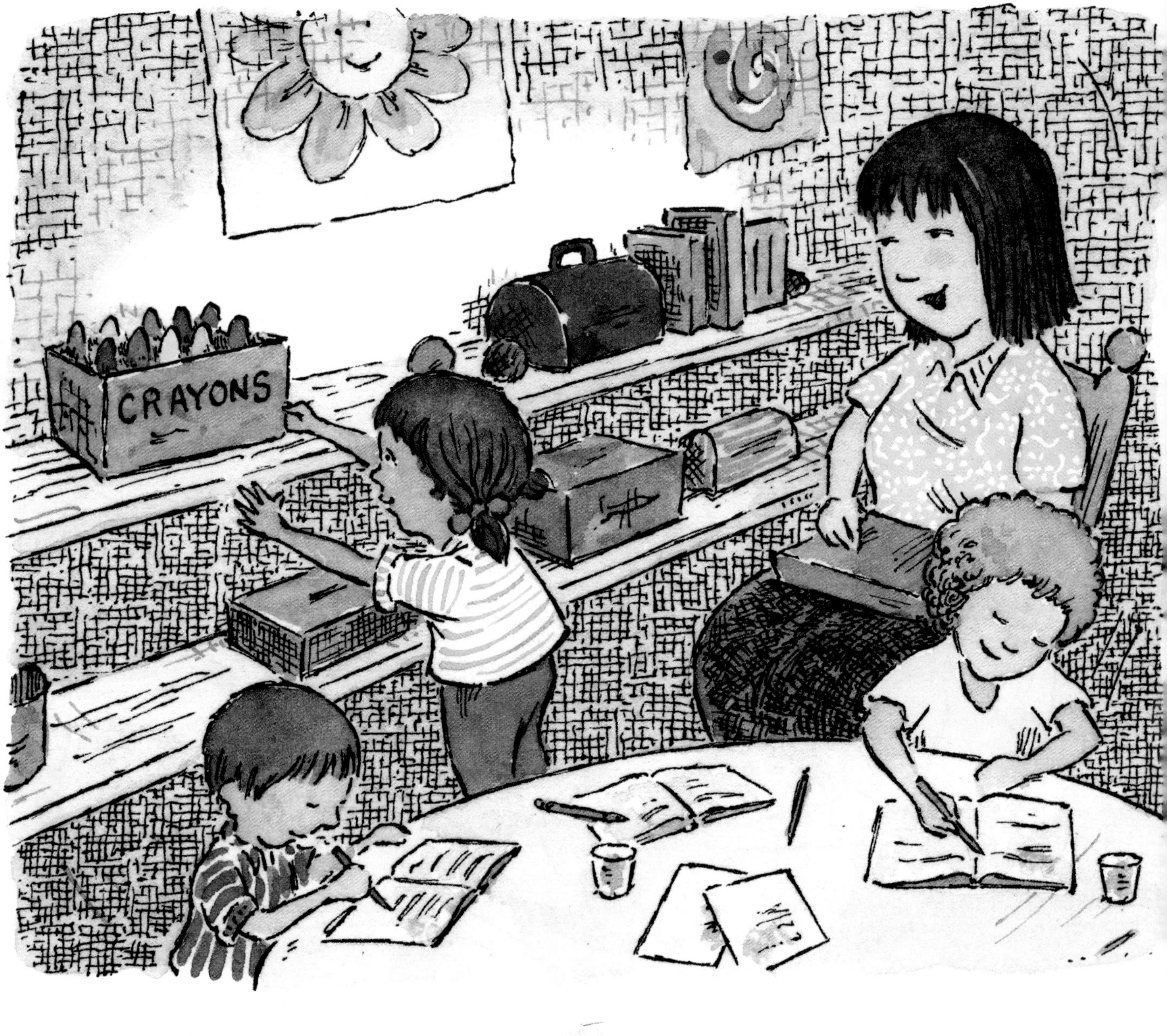

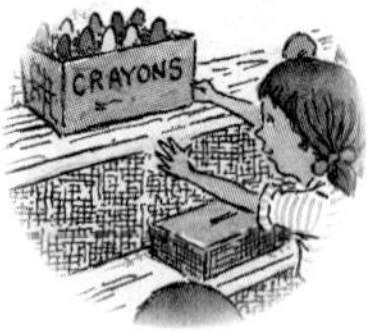

top

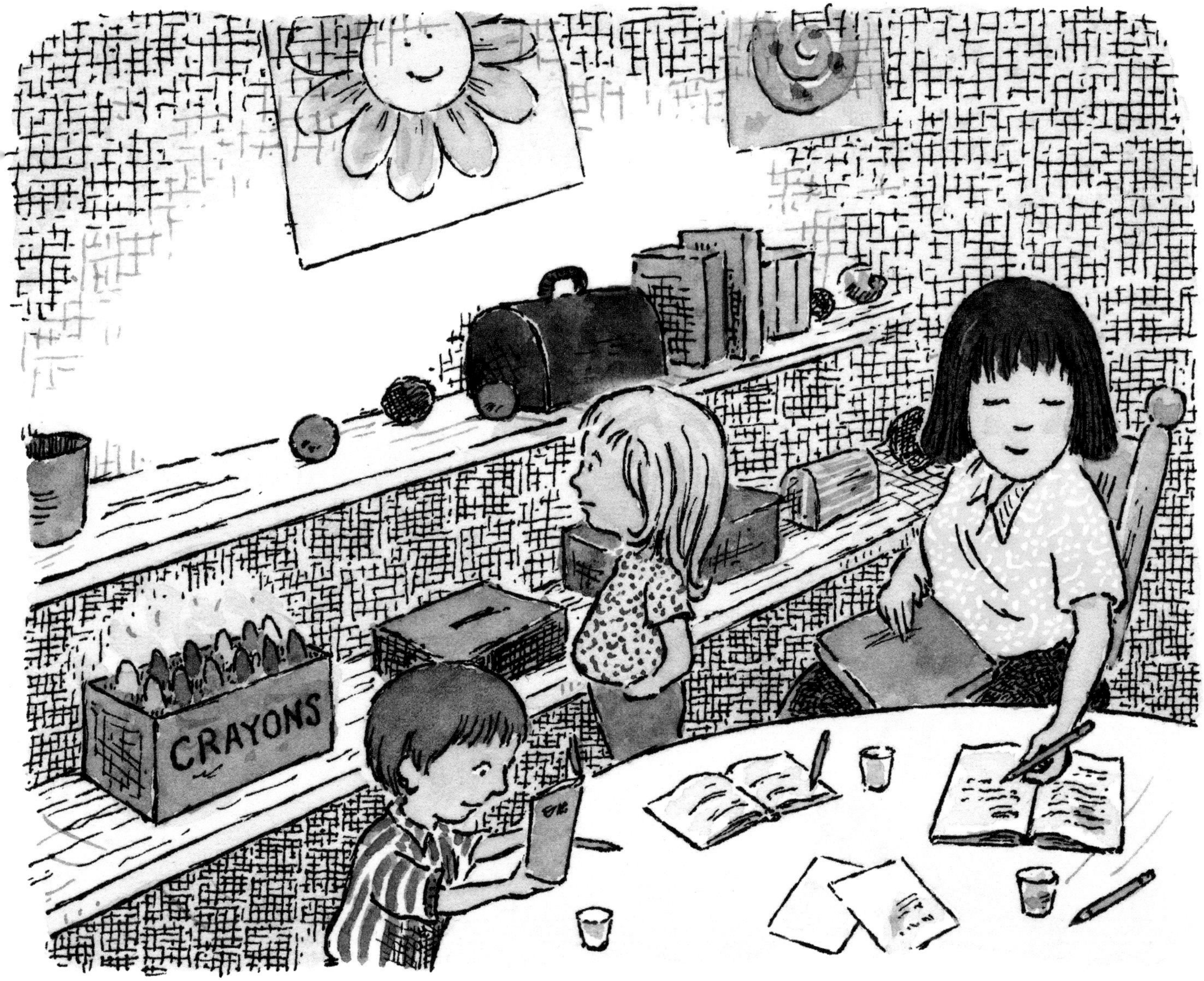

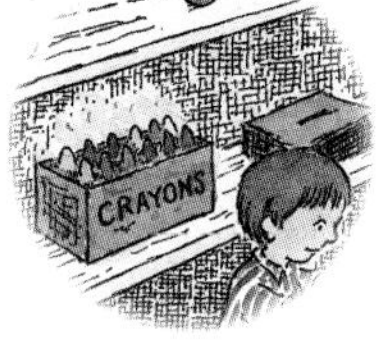

bottom

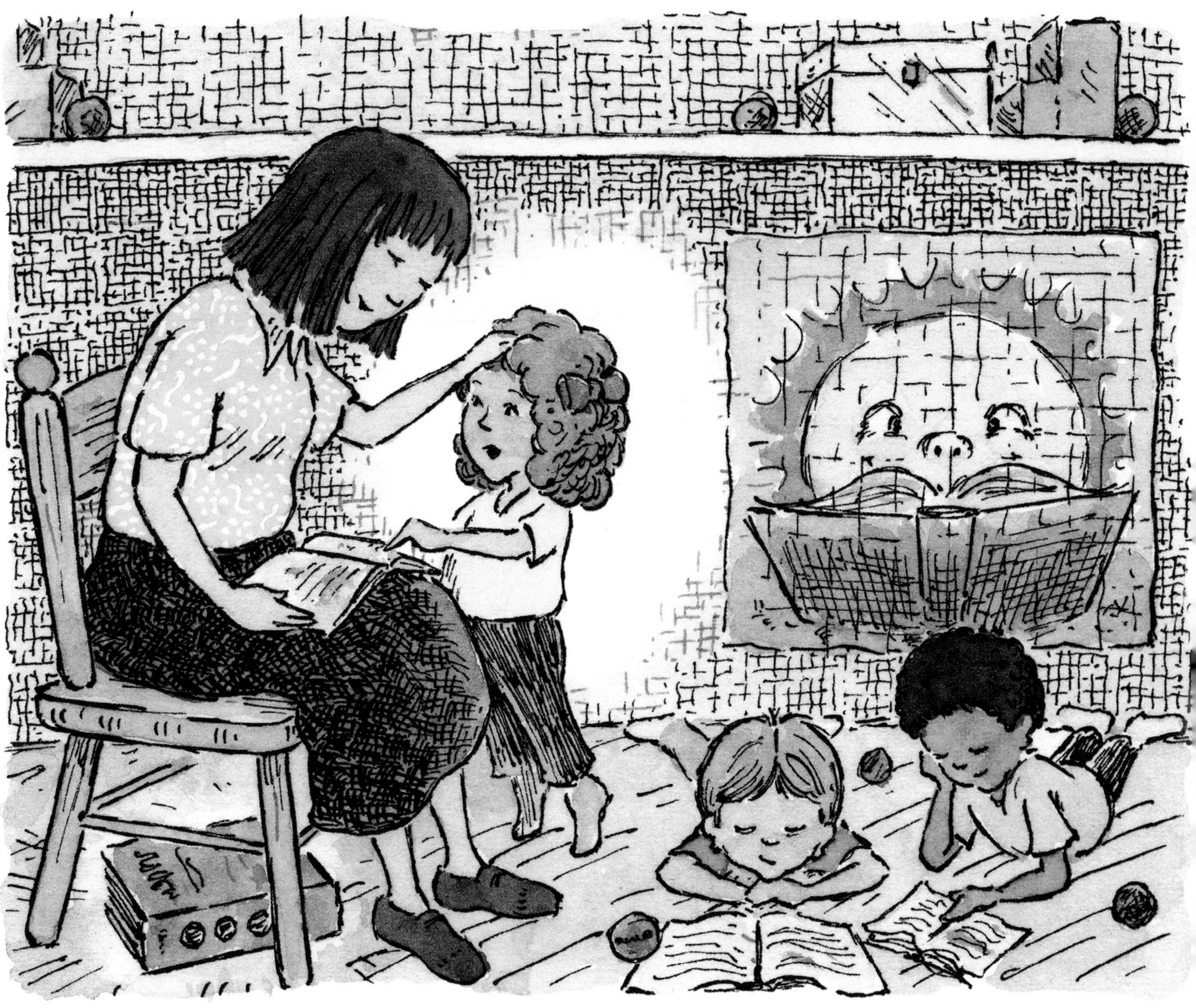

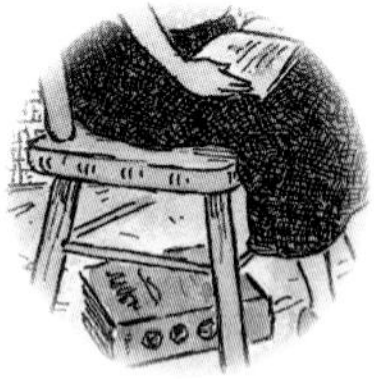

under

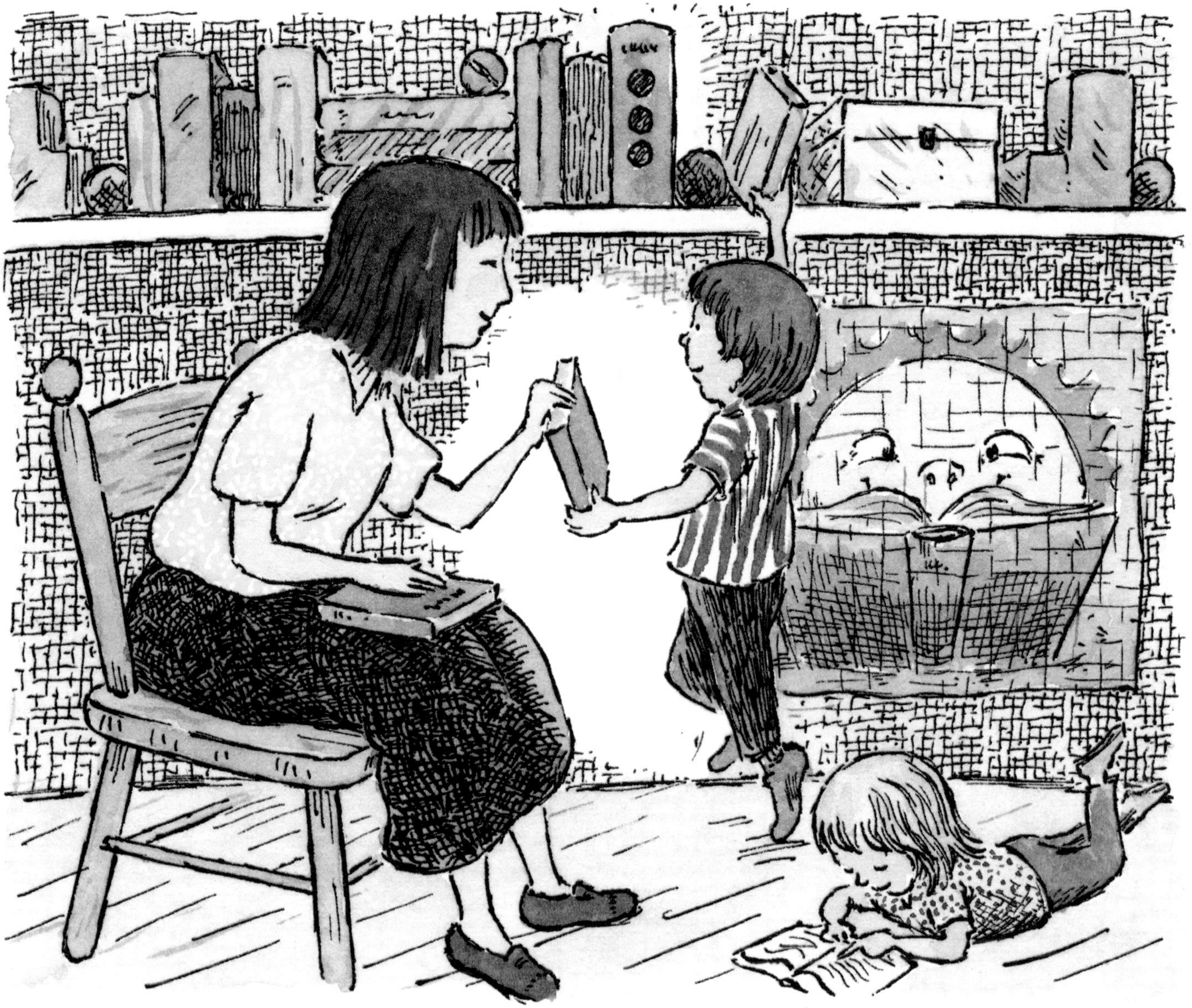

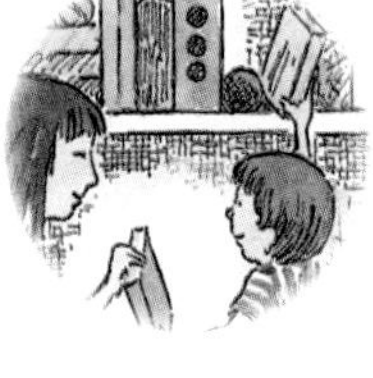

over

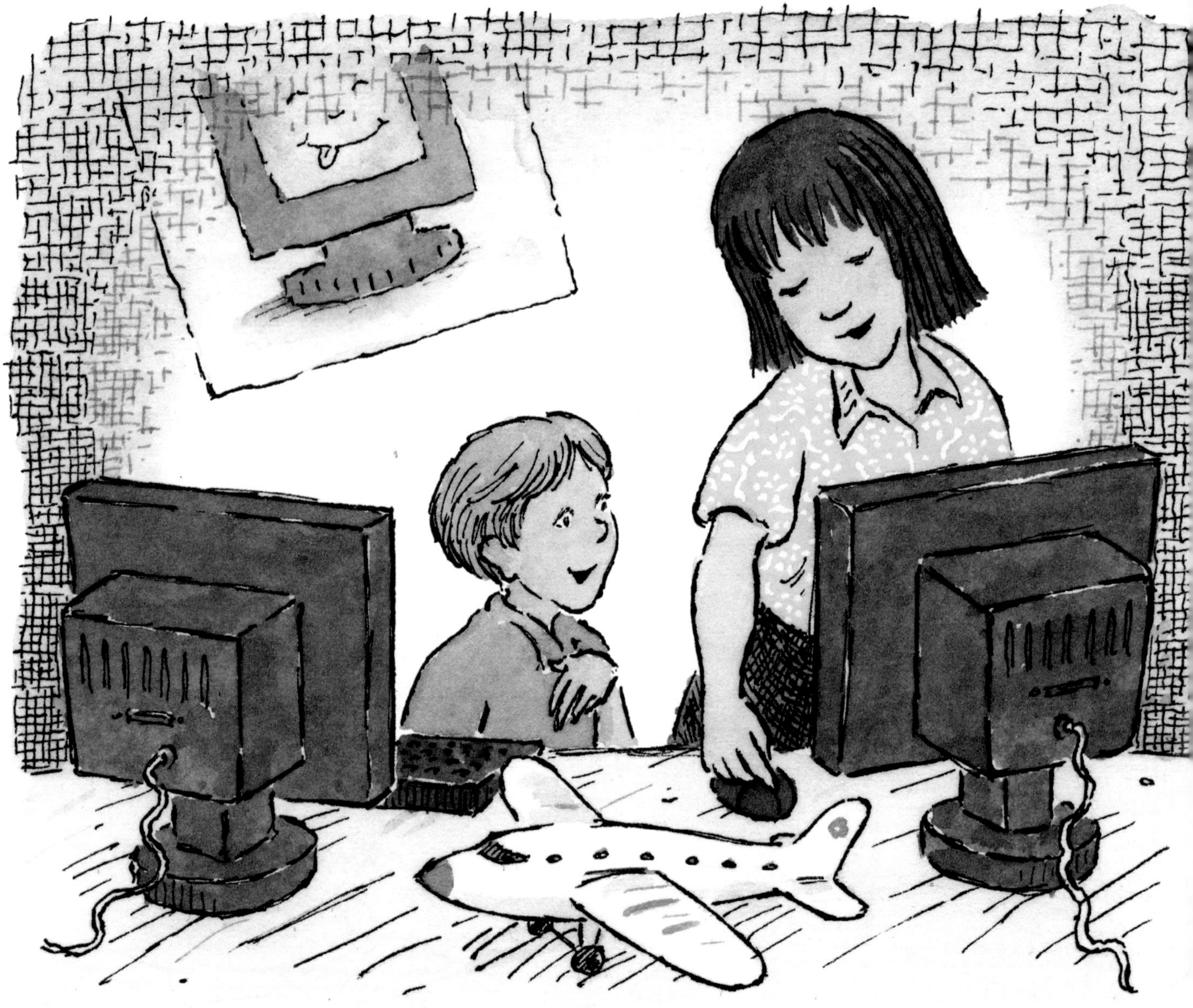

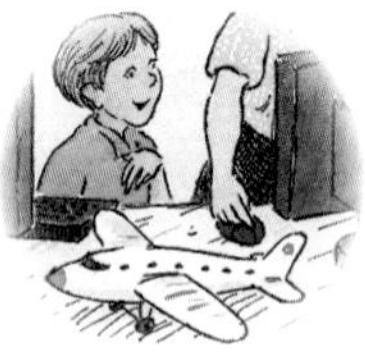

in between